DEMOCRACY AND DISCIPLINE

RITURAJ BASUMATARY | SWMAOSHAR BRAHMA

Copyright © Rituraj Basumatary, Swmaoshar Brahma
All Rights Reserved.

Contents

Preface

This book deals with Democracy and Discipline. Hope that the publication of this book will be useful. This book may not be free from errors and constructive criticisms are welcomed for the improvement of this book.

CHAPTER I

Introduction

Democracy is mainly a Greek word which means people and their rules, here peoples are having rights to select their own government as per their choice. Greece was the first democratic country in the world. India is a democratic country where people select their government on own choice, also people have the rights to do their work on their choice. There are two types of democracy direct and representative and hybrid or semi-direct democracy. There are many decisions which are made under democracies. People enjoy few rights which are very essential for human beings to live happily. Our country having the largest democracy. In a democracy, each people have equal rights to fight for the development. After the independence, India has adopted democracy, where the people vote those who are above 18 years of age, but these vote does not vary any caste all caste people have equal rights to select their government. India is the largest democratic country where a lot of problems faces which do not follow efficiently function. Democracy also called as a rule of the majority, means whatever the majority of people deciding it has to follow or implemented, the representative winning with the more number of votes will have the power. We can say the place where literacy people are more there it shows the success of the democracy even lack of consciousness is also dangerous in a democracy. Democracy is associated with higher human accumulation and higher economic freedom. Democracy is closely tied with the economic source of growth like education and quality of life as well as health care. The constituent assembly in India was adopted by Dr B.R. Ambedkar on 26th November 1949 and became sovereign democratic after its constitution came into effect on 26 January 1950.

CHAPTER II

What are the Challenges

There are many challenges for democracy like- corruption here many political leaders and officers who don't do work with integrity every place they demand bribes, results in the lack of trust on the citizens which affects the country very badly. Anti-social elements- which are seen during elections where people are given bribes and they are forced to vote a particular candidate. Caste and community- where a large number of people give importance to their cast and community, therefore, the political party also select the candidate on the majority population of caste. We see where ever the particular caste people is more win the elections where he does good for the society or not, and in some cases, good leaders lose because of less count of the vote.

CHAPTER III

Principles of Democracy

There are mainly five principles like- republic, socialist, sovereign, democratic and secular, with all these quality political parties will contest for elections. There will be many bribes given to the needy person who require food, money, shelter and ask them to vote whom they want. But we can say that democracy in India is still better than the other countries.

Basically any country needs democracy for development and better functioning of the government. In some countries, freedom of political expression, freedom of speech, freedom of the press, are considered to ensure that voters are well informed, enabling them to vote according to their own interest.

CHAPTER IV

Merits of Democracy

In a democracy, better government forms because it is more accountable and on the interest of the people.

1. improves the quality of decision making and enhances the dignity of the citizens.
2. provide a method to deal with differences and conflicts.

A democratic system of government is a form of government in which supreme power is vested in the people and exercised by them directly or indirectly through a system of representation usually involving periodic free elections. It permits citizens to participate in making laws and public policies by choosing their leaders, therefore citizens should be educated so that they can select the right candidate for the ruling government. Also, there are some concerns regarding democracy- leaders always keep changing in democracy with the interest of citizens and on the count of votes which leads to instability. It is all about political competition and power, no scope for morality.

CHAPTER V

Factors Affecting Democracy

The factors affecting Democracy are-
   (1) culture
   (2) capital and civil society
   (3) economic development
   (4) equality
   (5) modernization.
Norway and Iceland are the best democracy country in the world India is standing on fifty-one position.

India is a parliamentary democratic republic where the President is head of the state and Prime minister is head of the government. The guiding principles of democracy such as protected rights and freedoms, free and fair elections, accountability and transparency of government officials, citizens have a responsibility to uphold and support their principles. Democracy was first practised in the 6th century BCE, in the city-state of Athens. One basic principle of democracy is that people are the source of all the political power, in a democracy people rule themselves and also respect given to diverse groups of citizens, so democracy required to select the government of their own interest and make the nation developed by electing good leaders.

Today, many people see democracy as under threat in a way that only a decade ago seemed unimaginable. Following the fall of the Berlin Wall in 1989, it seemed like democracy was the way of the future. But nowadays, the state of democracy looks very different; we hear about 'backsliding' and 'decay' and other descriptions of a sort of creeping authoritarianism. Some long-established democracies, such as the United States, are witnessing a violation of governmental norms once thought secure, and this has culminated in the recent insurrection at the US Capitol. If democracy is a torch that shines for a time before then burning out – think of Classical Athens and Renaissance city republics – it all feels as if we might be heading toward a new period of darkness. What can we do to reverse this apparent trend and support democracy?

First, we must dispense with the idea that democracy is like a torch that gets passed from one leading society to another. The core feature of democracy – that those who rule can do so only with the consent of the people – wasn't invented in one place at one time: it evolved independently in a great many human societies.

Over several millennia and across multiple continents, early democracy was an institution in which rulers governed jointly with councils and assemblies of the people. From the Huron (who called themselves the Wendats) and the Iroquois (who called themselves the Haudenosaunee) in the Northeastern Woodlands of North America, to the republics of Ancient India, to examples of city governance in ancient Mesopotamia, these councils and assemblies were common. Classical Greece provided particularly important instances of this democratic practice, and it's true that the Greeks gave us a language for thinking about democracy, including the word *demokratia* itself. But they didn't invent the practice. If we want to better understand the strengths and weaknesses of our modern democracies, then early democratic societies from around the world provide important lessons.

The core feature of early democracy was that the people had power, even if multiparty elections (today, often thought to be a definitive feature of democracy) didn't happen. The people, or at least some significant fraction of them, exercised this power in many different ways. In some cases, a ruler was chosen by a council or assembly, and was limited to being first among equals. In other instances, a ruler inherited their position, but faced constraints to seek consent from the people before taking actions both large and small. The alternative to early democracy was autocracy, a system where one person ruled on their own via bureaucratic subordinates whom they had recruited and remunerated. The word 'autocracy' is a bit of a misnomer here in that no one in this position ever truly ruled on their own, but it does signify a different way of organising political power.

Early democratic governance is clearly apparent in some ancient societies in Mesopotamia as well as in India. It flourished in a number of places in the Americas before European conquest, such as among the Huron and the Iroquois in the Northeastern Woodlands and in the 'Republic of Tlaxcala' that abutted the Triple Alliance, more commonly known as the Aztec Empire. It was also common in precolonial Africa. In all of these societies there were several defining features that tended to reinforce early democracy: small scale, a need for rulers to depend on the people for knowledge, and finally the ability of members of society to exit to other locales if they were unhappy with a ruler. These three features were not always present in the same measure, but collectively they helped to underpin early democracy.

To see how autocracy – the alternative to early democracy – functioned, we can find no better example than that of Imperial China. China's earliest historical dynasties, the Shang and the Zhou (from the 2nd and 1st millennia BCE), had kings who ruled through an army and a bureaucracy, and there is no evidence of councils or assemblies of the people. Autocracy has been a near-constant feature of rule in China, suggesting that it wasn't some aberration but instead simply a different path of political development from Western European societies. The culmination of the Chinese model, achieved during the Tang and Song dynasties (7th to 13th centuries CE), involved the incorporation of the political elite into the state via a system of meritocratic recruitment based on a civil service exam. The Chinese civil service exam – which Europeans with their weak states later marvelled at – served a purpose not so different from a parliament but in a fundamentally different way because it was not local people who chose the representatives.

Of course, a simple return to early democracy is neither possible nor desirable. But early democracy does help us better understand the frailties of the modern democratic experience. A closer look at early democracy can in turn help us to understand what we might do to see that democracy today fulfils the underlying idea of *demokratia*: bringing power to the people.

The first difference between early democracy and our democracies today is that this earlier form of rule was a small-scale phenomenon. In some cases, governance took place only at the level of a small community, as was the case with the Hidatsa, an Indigenous American group living on the banks of the upper Missouri River. When governance was local like this, councils tended to meet very frequently. In other instances, such as with the Mesopotamian Kingdom of Mari, a larger polity existed, but early democracy remained a local phenomenon practised through the assemblies of individual towns. These might meet to consider how taxes should be allotted. It was rarer to see an early democracy that had a larger-scale assembly that drew members from multiple locations as did the Huron confederacy. Even in that case, though the Huron moved over a large area, the territory of concentrated settlement remained compact, something like 56 km east to west, and 30 km north to south. Populations were similarly small compared with modern democracies, with the Huron confederacy composed of, roughly, only 20,000 individuals.

Small scale had a critical implication for the nature of politics; in Classical Athens, among the Hidatsa and in the Kingdom of Mari, those who had the right to participate in politics tended to do so in a very direct and intensive way, particularly in local assemblies. In modern democracy, participation is very broad – often broader than in early democracy – but it's also not deep; for most of us, it's limited to voting in elections every few years, and in between these moments others make the decisions. The potential risk of this arrangement, as has been noted by astute observers since the birth of modern republics, is that citizens might grow distrustful of the people who are actually running government on a daily basis and of the special influences to which they might be subject. It's worth noting that, among long-established democracies today, there's a robust correlation whereby countries with larger populations tend to have lower trust in government.

We need new investments that better connect citizens with government.

One way to address the problem of scale is to delegate much more power to states, provinces and localities. There are some today, such as the American political analyst Yuval Levin, who here invoke the principle of subsidiarity: devolve power to the lowest level that's practical. In some Western democracies, such as Canada, Germany or the US, the presence of a federal system ensures that this is already the case for many policies, but this strategy can go only so far. On crucial issues of foreign trade, diplomacy or pressing constitutional questions, for example, it's impractical for individual states, regions or provinces to set their own policy.

If we can't return to 'all politics is local', then one alternative is to see what could be done to better connect citizens with a distant state. Historically, one way this has happened is through investments in the diffusion of information.

The early republic in the US provides an important example of government investment to overcome the problem of scale. In 'Federalist Number 10' (1787), James Madison had written that a large republic would naturally suffer less turbulence than would a small one, but a few years after the ratification of the Constitution, he began to sing a very different tune. In an essay entitled 'Public Opinion', Madison wrote about the difficulty in a vast republic that people would have in informing themselves about government. So he advocated the subsidised distribution of newspapers, and this helped result in the passage of the Postal Service Act of 1792.

The world today is much different than it was in 1792; citizens, if they want to, can drown themselves in information and disinformation. This suggests that we need to think of new investments that might better connect citizens with government by giving them information sources that are in touch with reality and that, in the case of the US, would avoid fanning the flames of longstanding racism. In some countries, most notably the US and the United Kingdom, the local press, though known to be both more trusted and less partisan than national outlets, faces economic conditions that are leading to its disappearance. A subsidy for local news outlets could be money well spent, just as the subsidy that the US Congress voted in 1792 was appropriate.

If large scale has the potential to lead to distrust and disengagement in a democracy, then a closely related problem is that of polarisation. Polarisation can take many forms, such as that involving tensions between different classes of people in the same location, or a difference of opinions between people living in different locations. In a broad set of democracies today, polarisation has increasingly taken this latter form, with those in large, cosmopolitan urban centres acquiring an entirely different worldview from those elsewhere, whether they involve rural districts as in the US, or distant urban centres in the UK, or the contrast between more urban and western areas in Turkey and those areas further to the east. In many of these cases, political scientists have shown that polarisation is asymmetric, as those on the political Right have been the principal ones to move to the extremes. The problem of geographic polarisation was not unknown to people in early democracies, and they found creative ways of addressing it. While we can't simply copy the solutions they found, we can still certainly learn from them.

Consider the example of the reforms implemented by Cleisthenes in Athens beginning in the year 508 BCE. In the decades prior to this date, the Athenians had developed a collective form of governance with a Council of Four Hundred, which had been established by Solon earlier in the 6th century BCE. It was composed of 100 members from each of four historical tribes, which might have been primarily kin-based or occupation-based, depending on which source one considers. While this system provided equal representation for each tribe, to the extent that there was animosity between these groups – one might even say polarisation – the system of representation might have reinforced this tension. Seeking to change matters, upon assuming power in 508 BCE, Cleisthenes revamped Athenian society by doing away with the four traditional tribes and creating 10 new ones to replace them. Aristotle later recounted a crucial element of Cleisthenes' reform: he assigned individual local groups of people called *demes* by lot into each of the 10 new tribes, therefore 'intermixing the members' of the prior four tribes. Aristotle states further that Cleisthenes made sure that the new tribes weren't geographically concentrated; instead, each had *deme* membership from the city, the coast and the interior of the Attic Peninsula.

People in polarised societies today could learn something from the Iroquois clan system.

Importantly, the principle of Cleisthenes' reform is far from unique; we have eloquent examples of people in other early democracies across multiple continents doing more or less the same thing. To see this, we can return to examples of the Huron and the Iroquois societies, each of which was divided – much like the Athenians – into separate tribes, and clearly geographically demarcated. This might seem like a system that would be ripe for intertribal conflict. But the Huron and the Iroquois had an ingenious system to fight against localism and polarisation. They divided their society not only into tribes, composed of villages, but also into clans that cross-cut tribal divisions. So, if you were a member of the wolf clan in an individual village among the Cayuga tribe in the Iroquois confederacy, to take one example, then you had a natural affiliation with Cayuga members of that clan from other villages, and you also had a link to members of the wolf clan in other Iroquois tribes. The clear intent of this system was to better bind society together by mitigating polarisation along tribal lines.

CHAPTER VI

Discipline

The word discipline has been derived from the Latin word 'disciplina' which deals with the process of "instruction and training."

In general sense, discipline refers to the practices adapted by the people for leading towards right direction with the basis of certain standards of behavior and to control the behavior against any hoodwink or harsh activities.

In educational sense, discipline refers to the course of action taken by a teacher or by the educational institution towards a student when the student's behavior interrupts the existing academic activities or mislead the activities created by certain educational organization.

CHAPTER VII

Definitions of Discipline

Bryan S. Turner (2006) defined discipline as "a body of knowledge and knowledge for the body because the training of the mind has inevitably involved a training of the body and it signified a method of training or instruction in a body of knowledge."

According to **Michel Foucault (1975)**, "Discipline is a mechanism of power which regulates the behavior of individuals in the social body."

According to **Cambridge Dictionary**, " Discipline refers to the training that makes people more willing to obey or more able to control themselves, often in the form of rules and punishments if these are broken."

According to **Webster Dictionary**, "Discipline refers to punish or penalize for the sake of enforcing obedience, perfecting moral character and to train or develop by instruction and to bring under control."

Thus, one of the essential part of life includes discipline. It is melancholic in the sense that in this contemporary world, there are various factors which can even deteriorate the career of the students if they do not adhere to certain rules and regulations, cultural norms and ethical values. It is noteworthy, that school is to be considered as one of the first orientation where student learns to follow disciplines from their very initial level of education and it eventually helps them to mould their behavior in a desirable way.

CHAPTER VIII

Types of Discipline

The types of discipline that are followed in the process of education are as follows:

1. **Preventive Discipline:** Preventive discipline refers to certain measures taken by a teacher in order to refrains students from adopting any kind of inappropriate behavior by students at the earliest. For instance, students may be taught about do's and don't through adaptation of certain rules and regulations by the institutional authorities.

2. **Supportive Discipline:** This discipline can be regarded as an alternative way of preventive discipline. At this point of view, it refers to depict the right path to the students at the right time and at the right place. For instance, certain warnings may be given to a student in an attempt to any illegal activities carried out by a student.

3. **Corrective Discipline:** Corrective discipline may be taken when a student fails to show any kind of improvement in his behavior despite of numerous efforts at the prior disciplines i.e. including both preventive and supportive discipline. For example; punishment such as imposition of late fee, suspension from schools, etc.

CHAPTER IX

Features of Discipline

The salient features of discipline can be summarized as follows:

- **Negative Approach:** It is based on negative approach in an attempt to avoid undertaking any illegal and harsh course of action.
- **Efficiency of time management:** It entails completion of any certain task at an accurate time or being always punctual.
- **Focus:** It enables to stay focused towards a desirable goal.
- **Balancing:** It assists in terms of balancing three entities of ours existence, i.e. body, soul and spirit.
- **Self-control:** It includes 'self-controlling' of one's emotions to adopt certain organizational rules and regulations.
- **Commitment:** Discipline is all about keeping commitments that we make ourselves and others.

Thus, discipline is the process of enhancement and moulding the behaviors of individual and then it sets as an automatic sub- conscious action for the students.

CHAPTER X

Needs and Importance of Discipline

Discipline plays a crucial role in appraisal of the nation through the processes of education. The needs and importanceof discipline in the process of education are as follows:

1. Goal-oriented

It is a fact that a disciplined person can always focus in his work whatever he/she intends or desire to achieve in life. Moreover, *discipline enables students to perceive dexterity of knowledge and always keep them motivated towards their studies as well as in other fields of their life. The magnificent way to stay motivated is to set a desire goal in their mind and to struggle hard for it by writing down all the study goals that intended to achieve it in their life.* However, a person being indiscipline may not be able to focus towards a particular goal and furthermore it may only deviate his attention towards an unnecessary stimuli which may even hinder his life throughout indulging in some illegal activities like consumptions of Alcohol, drugs, etc which is quite common in this contemporary world with an adolescent stage and always leads towards a tremendous raise in delinquency rate.

2. Inculcating of ethical values in students:

Inculcating of ethical values like humanity, honesty, self-discipline, not to hurt anyone, respect, justice, etc, were highly appreciated in gurukul system of education where the students tend to act morally and follow the societal guidelines. It is worth to be noted that inculcating of moral education is inevitable for the students in regard to cognizance of ethical values to be adopted in their most appropriate manner. But, in our present educational curriculum, provision of moral education has declined to a great extent due to which there has been tremendous rise in juvenile delinquency cases. According to the National Crime Records Bureau (NCRB) Report of 2015-2016, the data has shown that the total number of cases has been registered against juvenile in conflict with law and the case has increased from 18,939 to 31,396. Thus, from this point of view, it is clear that if moral education would have been given much value, there would have some declination in the proliferation of juvenile delinquency cases.

3. Professional ethics of the teacher: In an ancient period of education, teacher was given top-priority and was treated with deep respect and honour in the society. It is a fact that every teacher should be subjected to the code of ethical standards and must be guided by inner ethical code. By inner ethical code of conduct, here it means to reflect as a transparent and set as example to be of good personality in front of their students. Besides that, teachers used to treat every child equally. But, in present education system, some teachers often discriminate in grading system on the basis of caste, gender, religion, etc, due to overwhelming mass of the population across the country. It has been noticed in the study of Hanna & Linden (2012) while they intend to determine the discrimination in grading against low-caste children in India, they have reported through their study that the low-caste children were graded between 0.03 and 0.09 standard deviation below high caste children with the same answers of the students.

4. Providing a Stress-Free Environment

It is worth to be mentioning that when a student follows a certain discipline in life, it becomes quite efficient for them to remain on top of the things, i.e., either in their studies or intheir personal lives. A well-disciplined person finds it easier to be stress free because they do not face tension during exams or daily routine work. Staying disciplined helps them to study on time so that they are stress-free. Discipline helps in managing the work in a planned manner. Discipline also assists the students in maintaining stress-free and also prevents them from various mental illnesses like anxieties, stress, depression, etc.

5. Being both Physically and Mentally fit: Disciplined person always set up his/her mind to conduct daily regular exercises in order to maintain good physical health as there is a saying that "A healthy mind lives in a healthy body." They usually plan their schedule in such a way that it enables to enhance their academic performance as well as their physical health. Furthermore, a disciplined person can always easily determine the good and bad things for them in which it assists them in adopting,consumption of healthy foods habits, regular exercises, proper sleeping habits, waking up patterns,etc.

6. Excel in Academic Performance

Being disciplined is highly essential for better process of education. *Discipline* is obligatory in every student life because education is just incomplete without discipline. It further develops listening capabilities among students to listen to their teacher carefully and also helps them to understand the entire process of education. It is worthwhile in the sense that, if the students follow certain discipline, they are able to complete their given assignments task in due time. Moreover, if the *students* stay in the *discipline,* they are able to perform well in class and helps them to secure good marks in the examination as well. Along with getting good grades, students also learn a lot of new things being a disciplined student. There is no doubt that if the *students* stay in the *discipline*, they will become successful in their life and from which they will be benefited much for their establishment of career and in removing bewilder and perplexity in terms of choosing any appropriate career for their life.

7. Efficiency in Time Management

It is worth to be noted that if *students* follow the *discipline* meticulously then they can manage their time significantly. Moreover, adapting *appropriate discipline may* assists students in doing all kind of academic activities efficiently on time. But, if the student does not follow discipline in their life and in which they may spend their precious time by indulging themselves on extraneous activities beyond their academic relevant activities then they may suffer in their later life. Thus, students should adapt proper time table for their academic activities and should follow accordingly.

8. Connecting with Others

Being disciplined helps an individual to maintain a rich social network by flexing our communication skills. Additionally, it helps to develop a mutual relationship among parents, teachers, siblings, friends, etc rather than possessing any complexity in the relationship and thus it enables person to be much extrovert rather than to be introvert.

9. Understanding Oneself in a Better Sense

A disciplined person can be aware about one's natural or innate tendencies and enables him to determine as well as accept his/her strength and weaknesses in terms of one's capabilities towards undertaking any course of action. Thus, it leads them to have a pleasant experience about 'self-control'.

10. Enhancing Work life Balance:

It is a fact that each and every individual remains busy in their daily life activities which may sometimes leads towards stress or anxieties. Hence, being disciplined enables a person to balance their work life as well by indulging themselves in various recreational activities like gardening, participation in social programmes, etc, for the purpose of reducing stress in life and thereby such kind of recreational activities rendered by disciplined person may be helpful in balancing their work life.

11. Set as Good Examples to Others

It is highly imperative in the sense that students being disciplined also encourages or motivates other students of their class to be disciplined as well. On owing to this point of view, there is no denying the fact that theother students will definitely follow the students with discipline when they discern any positive impact on their academic performance as well as transcendence in other fields of their life.

CHAPTER XI

Role of Education in inculcating discipline

Education entails inculcating ethical values, optimism and contribution towards the society to bring positive changes in every aspects of human life. In the term of 'education' it includes a systematic curriculum to be followed for an overall development of the child in every perspective manner. In ancient period, gurukul system of education emerged in the Indian subcontinent reversed to around 5000 BC which was prevalent during the Vedic Period of education where students were practically taught about the various subjects with the help of a teacher or 'Acharya' and followed a strict discipline. It is futile in the sense that, if we look at the present scenario of the educational system of India, we could see a huge gap between the ancient and modern educational system since over the years there has been a tremendous changes in the system of education. It is thus evident that ancient gurukul system of education had enriched in values and focused more on all round development of the child as compared to modern Education is the most basic thing in the life of human being to acquire knowledge and experience. It is obvious that it can be acquired through the process of teaching and learning from the grass root level in the educational institutions. Through the process of education, we accumulate knowledge about various things in an around the world. In Ancient India, education was taught in a traditional way which is also known as Gurukul system of education. It was a residential schooling system during the Vedic Period reversed to around 5000 BC. In this system, students were taught various things like culture, discipline and lots more. In this education system, they had a teacher (Acharya) and students (shisya) where they used to reside under the same roof. The teacher and students thereby develops a mutual rclationship while residing in Guru's residence and the teacher do not charge them for the admission of the students but they have to give them as 'gurudakshina' as consideration at the completion of their course. It is worth to mentioning that, here the students do not only learn about language and disciplines but also about various subjects such as crafts, sports, arts, singing and they perform yoga, meditation, mantra, chanting for positivity. Besides that, it also helps students to be confident, mindful disciplined and intellectual which is substantial for the livelihood of modern educational system.

CHAPTER XII

Conclusion

People in polarised societies today could learn something from the Iroquois clan system and the 10 Athenian tribes. As we become ever more tribal in nature in countries such as the US, perhaps we could learn more from societies that actually had tribes. The lesson wouldn't be to establish new tribes or clans of our own: it would be, instead, to examine how different political and social institutions can aid in creating links for people living in different places, from different backgrounds and holding very different beliefs. The idea here would be to help strengthen and unify society by creating new links across the lines of polarisation.

The absence of a state bureaucracy was a chief reason why early democracy proved to be such a stable form of rule for so many societies. With little autonomous power – apart from the ability to persuade – those who would have liked to rule as autocrats found themselves without the means to do so. The flipside of this was that, in many early democracies, those who were unhappy with a central decision could simply refuse to participate or even decamp to a new locality. It was much like many online communities today where those at the centre, sometimes called 'benevolent dictators for life', have no option to rule as autocrats because they depend upon input and services provided by individuals who could simply refuse to participate or move elsewhere.

Modern democracy lacks the same protections from central power that early democracies enjoyed. At the same time, having a powerful central state can allow a society to achieve goals such as universal education and prosperity, to name but a few. The question then is how to live with a state while preserving democracy. Doing so involves remaining vigilant about the encroachment of central state power rather than hoping that a country's constitution alone might provide adequate protection, most notably in the case of the US where the document was laid out at a now-distant founding moment.

Those who debated the US Constitution of 1787 recognised the danger posed by an encroaching central state. The compromise they achieved resulted in an extensive series of checks and balances designed to enable state power while also restraining it. The administration of the former US president Donald Trump demonstrated just how much executive power could run rampant in spite of all the intended safeguards. In some eastern European countries, a similar pattern has taken place and even gone much further. In the 1990s, it was believed that the checks and balances safeguarding democracy would involve membership in the European Union and adhesion to its extensive set of supranational rules, yet in this decade the Fidesz party in Hungary and their Law and Justice counterparts in Poland have demonstrated that it's possible to break a great many democratic norms – and in fact rewrite the formal rules – without having EU membership serve as an effective backstop. The lesson from all of these cases would seem to be that, while designing a constitution well is an important thing, after that point maintaining a healthy democracy in the face of executive power requires constant vigilance, and perhaps more vigilance than we had been used to paying until late.